Linda —

In Peace

With love

Lewis

RUMI

A Spiritual Treasury

RUMI

A Spiritual Treasury

COMPILED BY JULIET MABEY

ONEWORLD

OXFORD

RUMI: A SPIRITUAL TREASURY

Oneworld Publications
(Sales and Editorial)
185 Banbury Road
Oxford OX2 7AR
England
http://www.oneworld-publications.com

Oneworld Publications
(US Office)
237 East 39th Street
New York
NY10016

ISBN 1–85168–215–5

Cover and text design by Design Deluxe, Bath
Printed by Graphicom Srl, Vicenza, Italy

CONTENTS

INTRODUCTION

JALAL AL-DIN Rumi (1207–73 CE) was born in thirteenth-century Persia, in an area that is today part of Afghanistan. His family fled their native Khurasan as Mongols gathered to invade, and eventually settled in Konya, in present-day Turkey, also known as Rum – hence the name, Rumi. The son of a well-known Sufi preacher and jurisprudent, Baha Walad, he was trained from an early age in traditional Islamic fields, and later in the ways of Sufism, the mystical branch of Islam. On the death of his father in 1231, Rumi took on his role as a preacher and doctor of the law, and followed the Sufi practices of the spiritual path. However, in 1244, Rumi encountered a mysterious wandering dervish, Shams-i Tabrizi, and his spiritual world underwent a major revolution.

Shams was to prove Rumi's inspiration, leading him to the zenith of mystical experience. For two years they were inseparable, but then Shams vanished, never to be seen again. Some say that grief over this loss caused Rumi to institute the legendary religious dance – or whirling – among his followers, later to be referred to as the Whirling Dervishes. In many of Rumi's poems he speaks of his love for Shams; the figure of Shams is used as an analogy for God, the pain of separation from Shams representing the pain of Rumi's separation from, and longing for unity with, God. After Sham's disappearance, Rumi gave up his public preaching to devote himself to training his Sufi disciples and producing the vast outpouring of mystical poems that have brought him recognition as one of the greatest literary and spiritual figures of all time.

The selections in this short anthology have been chosen to demonstrate the breadth, in both style and range of subject matter, of Rumi's spiritual writings, and are drawn largely from Rumi's great works of poetry, the *Masnavi* (or *Mathnawi*) and the *Divan-i Shams*. The first is an epic narrative poem of 25,000 rhyming couplets, written in Persian over the last fifteen years of Rumi's life. Referred to as the "Qur'an of Persia," and widely regarded as the greatest spiritual masterpiece ever written, it is composed in a largely colloquial, didactic style. Combining explanations of the main themes of Sufi mystical life and doctrine, with a mixture of illustrative tales, parables, and analogies, it may be regarded as a spiritual handbook guiding the reader along the Sufi path to God. A manual of simple yet profound wisdom, the *Masnavi* expresses such power of thought and language that it remains, seven hundred years after it was first painstakingly dictated, as breathtaking as it was during the poet's own lifetime.

His other major work, the *Divan* (meaning "collection"), comprises the remainder of Rumi's poems, amounting to some 35,000 or more verses of shorter lyric poetry in the form of *ghazals*, *tarjiy'at*, and quatrains or *ruba'iyyat*. This collection spans thirty years of work, from the arrival of Shams until Rumi's death. Compared to the relatively sober *Masnavi*, the individual poems in the *Divan* are more ecstatic in nature; an outpouring of rapturous emotion frequently depicting intoxication with the love of God, and speaking of the deepest longings of the human heart. One third of these verses are addressed to Shams, and Rumi's outstanding achievement lies in his transformation of the passion of human love into a mirror for union with the divine.

A few quotations have been drawn from Rumi's prose work, *Fihi ma fihi*. Also written during his later years, this work is based on talks Rumi gave to his disciples. Didactic in nature, like the *Masnavi* it uses analogies to explain Sufi teachings.

The Sufi path is one of striving for spiritual perfection through the transformation of self, in order to draw nearer to God, who is perfection. Thus the primary goal of the Sufi is to transcend or "naught" the self or ego, which acts as a barrier or "veil" between the human heart and God, distorting our perception of reality and inhibiting our capacity to mature to our full "selfhood" in which we perfectly reflect the attributes of God. The focus is therefore on turning the soul to God; on becoming God-centered rather than self-centered; on the spiritual rather than the material, transitory world; and on inner, spiritual change rather than on the external reality of worldly status and wealth.

Progress along this "path" depends on love of God and the spiritual battles (or "holy war") that one must engage in to "polish the mirror of the heart," and thereby achieve the clarity of vision necessary truly to "see" our self and spiritual reality. This may bring us suffering in this world, but it leads to greater happiness in the world beyond, while pausing on the path to take one's comfort and ease in this physical world leads to great suffering in the next. Rumi also uses the analogy of the furnace to represent this process of spiritual transformation, where the rusty iron of our hearts is tempered and purified and polished until the reflection of the "Unseen" is beheld clearly within. To perfectly reflect the image of God in one's heart is to achieve union with Him.

This small anthology can do little more than offer a taste of Rumi's mystical vision. Anyone wishing to know more about Rumi should consult Franklin Lewis's excellent and exhaustive biography, which offers a very comprehensive account of his life, times and thought. Rumi's popularity has not dimmed with age – his work is read more widely today than ever before, inspiring readers of all faiths and creeds. In an increasingly secular and often troubled age, this humble Sufi ascetic offers a touch of wonder as he unfurls the possibility of divine love, guiding the reader along the path of spiritual growth with passion, patience and unflinching clarity.

JULIET MABEY

TOUCHING THE
DIVINE

If the thirsty drink water from a cup, they will see God in it.
Those who are not intoxicated with the love of God will see
only their own faces in it.

BECOMING A LOVER OF GOD

A LOVER never seeks without being sought by his
   beloved.
When the lightning bolt of love has pierced *this* heart,
   be assured that there is love in *that* heart.
When the love of God grows in your heart, beyond any
   doubt God loves you.

MASNAVI III:4393–6

OUR DESIRE for God is fanned by His love: it is His attraction that draws all wayfarers along the path. Does dust rise up without a wind? Does a ship float without the sea?

MASNAVI V:4216–17

O HEART, if you recognize any difference
Between joy and sorrow,
You will be torn apart.
Although what you desire tastes sweet,
Doesn't the Beloved desire you
To be desireless?
O, the life of lovers lies in death:
You will not win the Beloved's heart
Unless you lose your own.

MASNAVI I:1747–8; 1751

SOMEONE ASKED, "What is love?" God answered, "You will know when you lose yourself in Me."

MASNAVI II:PROLOGUE

WHEN THE pain of love increases your spiritual joy,
Roses and lilies fill the garden of your soul.

MASNAVI II:1379

THE RELIGION of Love transcends all other religions: for lovers, the only religion and belief is God.

MASNAVI II:1770

YOU ARE my sky, and I am the earth, bewildered:
What makes You constantly flow from my heart?
I am soil with parched lips! Bring kindly water
That will transform this soil into a rosebed!
How does the earth know what You sowed in its heart?
You have impregnated it, and You know its burden!

DIVAN-I SHAMS 3048

THE WATER said to the dirty one, "Come here."
The dirty one said, "I am too ashamed."
The water replied, "How will your shame be washed
   away without me?"

MASNAVI II:1366–7

LOVE OF God is rooted in our knowledge of God. When did ignorance lead to true love? Such ignorance is the cause of our banishment and prevents us drawing near to Him.

MASNAVI II:1532–3; 1538

ALL KINGS are enslaved to their slaves, all people are ready to die for one who dies for them. The hearts of lovers are captivated by those who have lost their hearts to them. Whoever you regard as a lover, know he is also beloved. And we who are God's beloved must become His lovers.

MASNAVI I:1736; 1739–40

THAT VOICE which is the origin of every cry and sound is, indeed, the only Voice; the rest are mere echoes.

MASNAVI I:2107

THE HOUSE of the heart into which the rays of the divine sun cannot reach is dark and destitute: it is bleak and cramped, its door remains closed. It is like a tomb. Come! Arise from the tomb of your heart!

MASNAVI II:3129–32

O, MAKE me thirsty, do not give me water!
Make me your lover! Banish my sleep!

DIVAN-I SHAMS 1751

WHETHER WE are sane or mad, we are intoxicated with
    the Cupbearer and the cup.
We bow our heads in submission to His word and His laws,
And willingly give up our lives to be pawns in His hand.
As long as the Friend is in our hearts, our only wish is
    to give up our lives in service to Him.

MASNAVI II:2571–3

DID I not tell you, "Do not leave, for I am your friend!"?
For in this mirage of nothingness I am the
  Fountainhead of Life!
Even if in anger you leave Me for a hundred thousand
  years,
In the end you will return, for I am your true Goal!

Did I not tell you, "Be not content with worldly
  forms!"?
For I am the fashioner of the tabernacle of your
  contentment!
Did I not tell you, "I am the Sea and you are but a
  single fish"?
Do not be tempted ashore, for I am your Crystal Sea!

Did I not tell you, "Do not fly like a bird to the
  snare!"?
Come to Me, for I am the very Power of your flight!
Did I not tell you, "They will rob you and leave you
  numb with cold"?
But I am the Fire and Warmth and Heat of your desire!

Did I not tell you, "They will taint your character,
Until you forget that I am your Source of Purity"?
Did I not tell you, "Do not question how I direct your
    affairs!"?
For I am the Creator without directions.

If your heart is a lamp, let it lead you to your true
    path.
And if you are godly, know that I am your Lord!

DIVAN-I SHAMS 1725

FOR THE lovers of God, He alone is the source of all joy and sorrow. He alone is the true object of desire; every other kind of love is idle infatuation. Love for God is that flame which, when it blazes, burns away everything except God. Love for God is a sword which cuts down all that is not of God. God alone is eternal; all else will vanish.

MASNAVI V:586–90

WHATEVER IS the object of your desire,
Go, absorb yourself in that beloved,
Assume its shape and qualities.

If you wish for the light, prepare yourself
To receive it; if you wish to be far from God,
Increase your egotism and drive yourself away.

And if you wish to find a way out of this ruined prison,
Do not turn your head away from the Beloved,
But bow in worship and draw near.

MASNAVI I:3605–7

MY HEART has become a pen
    in the Beloved's fingers:
Tonight He may write a *Z*,
    perhaps tomorrow, a *B*.
He cuts and sharpens His pen well
    to write in *riqaʿ* and *naskh*;
The pen says, "Lo, I obey,
    for You know best what to do."

DIVAN-I SHAMS 2530

THROUGH LOVE, the bitter becomes sweet;
Through love, copper becomes gold;
Through love, dregs become clear;
Through love, pains become healing;
Through love, the dead become living;
Through love, the king becomes a slave.

MASNAVI II:1529–31

O HELP of all those who call for help,
    lead us aright!
Do not let any heart stray
    that you have guided by Your grace
Do not sever us from all those
    who are well-pleased with You.
Nothing is more bitter to our taste
    then separation from You.
Without Your protection
    all is confusion.
The material world
    saps our spiritual strength.
Our bodies strip the cloth
    of spirituality from our souls.
How can we save our souls
    without Your help?
The soul that is not united with its Beloved
    is lost and miserable for ever.
If You do not admit a soul to Your presence,
    even alive, regard it as dead!
If You reproach Your slaves,
    that is only fitting, Lord.

And if You say the sun and moon are filth,
And if You declare the tall cypress bent,
And if You call the skies above contemptible,
And the seas and mines empty,
You speak the truth,
For You are the source of all perfections,
You alone have the power to perfect,
You are holy and free from non-existence,
You endow the non-existent with existence,
And bring them to life!

MASNAVI I:3899–912

SEEKING GOD

PLUG YOUR low sensual ear, which stuffs like cotton
Your conscience and makes deaf your inner ear.
Be without ear, without sense, without thought,
And hearken to the call of God, "Return!"
Our speech and action is the outer journey,
Our inner journey is above the sky.
The body travels on its dusty way;
The spirit walks, like Jesus, on the sea.

MASNAVI I:566–71

EVERY BLIND wayfarer, whether righteous or wicked,
God is dragging, bound in chains, into His presence.
All are dragged along this way reluctantly, save those
who are acquainted with the mysteries of divine
action.
The command "Come against your will" is addressed
to the blind follower; "Come willingly" is for the
man molded of truth.
While the former, like an infant, loves the nurse for the
sake of milk, the other has given his heart away to
this Veiled One.
The "infant" has no knowledge of her beauty: he wants
nothing of her except milk;
The real lover of the Nurse is disinterested, single-
minded in pure devotion.
Whether God's seeker loves Him for something other
than He, that he may continually partake of His
bounty,
Or whether he loves God for His Very Self, for naught
besides Him, lest he be separated from Him,
In either case the search proceeds from that Source:
the heart is made captive by that Heart-ravisher.

MASNAVI III:4581–3; 4590–600

KNOW THAT the outward form passes away,
But the world of reality remains for ever.
How long will you play at loving the shape of the jug?
Leave the jug; go, seek the water!

MASNAVI II:1020–1

THE SUNBEAM fell upon the wall;
The wall received a borrowed splendor.
Why set your heart on a piece of turf,
O simple one? Seek out the Source
Which shines for ever.

MASNAVI II:708–9

GOD HAS planted in your heart the desire to search for Him. Do not look at your weaknesses but focus on the search. Every seeker is worthy of this search. Strive to redouble your efforts, so that your soul may escape from this material prison.

MASNAVI V:1733–5

WHETHER YOU are fast or slow, eventually you will find what you are seeking. Always devote yourself wholeheartedly to your search. Even though you may limp or be bent double, do not abandon your search, but drag yourself ever toward Him.

MASNAVI III:978–80

WHEN A lamp has derived its light from a candle, everyone who sees the lamp certainly sees the candle. Either behold the light of God from the lamps of the saints, or behold His light from the candle of those who have gone before.

MASNAVI I:1947;1950

EVERY PROPHET and every saint has a way,
But all lead to God. All ways are really one.

MASNAVI I:3086

THERE IS a famous river, full of the water of life. Come, O heedless, thirsty one! Draw the water, so that the garden of your spirit may be nourished. If you cannot see the water of life; let religious teachers guide you to the stream where it flows. Then blindly dip a jug into it, and when it becomes heavy, you will know that some water has gone from the river to the jug. Time is passing by, and the abundant water is flowing away. Drink ere, through your unrequited thirst, you fall to pieces!

MASNAVI III:4301–8; 4300

PROPHETS AND religious teachers are like signs on the road, to guide spiritual travelers who become lost in the desert. But those who have attained union with God need nothing but their inner eye and the divine lamp of faith; they need no signs or even a road to travel along. Such people then become signs for others.

MASNAVI II:3312–14

UNTIL THE cloud weeps,
  how can the garden flourish?
Until the baby cries,
  how can the milk flow?
A newborn baby understands:
  if she cries, a nurse will come.
But the Nurse of all nurses
  only gives milk when you cry out.

MASNAVI V:134–6

THE REFLECTION cast from good friends is needed
Until you become, without the aid of any reflector,
A drawer of water from the sea.
Know that at first the reflection is just imitation,
But when it continues to recur,
It turns into direct realization of truth.
Until it has become realization,
Do not part from the friends who guide you –
Do not break away from the shell
Until the raindrop has become a pearl.

MASNAVI II:566–8

IF YOU have a touchstone, choose; otherwise, go and devote
yourself to one who is discerning. Either you must have a
touchstone within your own soul or, if you do not know the
way, find a guide.

MASNAVI II:746–7

YOUR EARTHLY beloved eclipses
　　the face of the Divine;
Your worldly guide drowns out
　　the words of your true spiritual guide.
Do not despair: make yourself cheerful,
　　call for help to Him who comes to the call.

MASNAVI I:3245; 3252

TURN BACK from existence toward non-existence,
If you seek the Lord and belong to the Lord.
Non-existence is the place of income;
Do not run away from it.
This existence of more or less
Is the place of expenditure.

MASNAVI II:688–9

WHILE THE thirsty seek water,
The water also seeks the thirsty.

MASNAVI I:1741

THE SENSUOUS eye is a horse,
And the light of God is the rider:
Without the rider the horse is useless.
The light of God rides the sensuous eye,
And then the soul yearns for God.
How can a riderless horse
Recognize the signs of the road?
God's light enhances the senses:
This is the meaning of "light upon light."

MASNAVI II:1286; 1290–3

REMEMBRANCE OF God instills in us a desire for the journey, and makes us into travelers.

DIVAN-I SHAMS 33569

THE PROPHET reported that God said,
"I am not contained in the container of high and low.
I am not contained in the earth nor in all the heavens.
But I am contained in the heart of My faithful servant.
How wonderful! If you seek Me, seek Me there."

MASNAVI I:2653–5

UNION WITH THE BELOVED

WE ARE the flute, our music is all Yours;
We are the mountain echoing only You;
Pieces of chess, You marshall us in line
And move us to defeat or victory;
Lions emblazoned high on flags unfurled –
Your wind invisible sweeps us through the world.

MASNAVI I:599–604

YOU ARE not really a hunter, seeking Me,
Instead, you are My slave and lie at My feet.
You devise means to attain my presence
But you are helpless either to leave or to seek Me.

The search for Me causes you anguish;
Last night I heard your heavy sighs.
It is within my power to end your waiting
To show you the Way and grant access.

So that you may be released from this whirlpool of time,
And may at last set foot on the treasure of union with Me,
But the sweetness and delights of the resting-place
Are in proportion to the pain endured on the journey.

Only when you suffer the pangs and tribulations of exile
Will you truly enjoy your homecoming.

MASNAVI III:4152–8

NEARNESS TO God cannot be calculated. To be near to God is not to go up or down, but to escape from the prison of existence. The treasure of God lies in non-existence. You are deluded by existence. How could you understand what non-existence is?

MASNAVI III:4513–16

WHAT DOES it mean to learn the knowledge of God's
    unity?
To consume yourself in the presence of the One.
If you wish to shine like the midday sun,
Burn up the darkness of self-existence.
Dissolve yourself in the Being of Him who is the
    Sustainer of all.
You have held fast to "I" and "we,"
And this dualism is your spiritual ruin.

MASNAVI I:3009–12

HAVE MERCY on all who have beheld Your face: how can we endure the bitterness of separation from You? You speak of separation and banishment: do what You will, but stay close to me! A hundred thousand deaths are preferable to separation from Your face. To die in the sure hope of union with God is a sweet prospect; but to live with the bitterness of banishment from God is to be consumed by fire.

MASNAVI V:4113–17

MY HEART is like a scroll
    that extends without end to Eternity,
Inscribed from first to last,
    "Do not leave me!"

DIVAN-I SHAMS 23493

HOLD TIGHTLY to the Perfect Moon
If you are a piece of the moon.
Why does a part keep aloof from its whole?

MASNAVI II:2580–1

THE SNOW constantly murmurs, "I will melt, become a
    torrent,
I will flow toward the sea, for I am part of the ocean!
I was alone, I was frozen solid,
And by affliction's jaws was crushed like ice!"

DIVAN-I SHAMS 1033

HE SPOKE, "You have given me a long life,
    and given me ample time,
You have given so many favors
    to one so lowly, God!
For seventy long years
    I have sinned here –
Yet not for one day did You withhold
    Your bounty from me!
Now I earn nothing;
    today I am Your guest,
I'll play the harp for You,
    for I am Yours!"

MASNAVI I:2083–5

EVERYTHING PERISHES except God's essence.
When you have died to yourself and become immersed
In His essence, you will never perish.
Whoever says "I" and "we" at the door
Of the divine court will be turned back:

One day a young man knocked at a friend's door.
"Who are you, O trusted one?" asked the friend.
He answered, "I!" The friend said, "Go away.
This is not the time for you to enter;
There is no place at my table for the raw!"
What, then, will cook the raw and so save him
But separation's fire and exile's flame?
The poor man left to travel a whole year
And burned with fire in exile from his friend,
And burning, he was cooked, and so returned,
And once again drew near to the friend's house.
He knocked at the door in great fearfulness
Lest from his lips discourteous words might fall.
His friend called out, "Who stands outside my door?"
He answered, "'Tis *you* at the door, O friend."
He replied, "Come in, now that you are I –
There is no room in this house for two 'I's!"

MASNAVI I:3052–3; 3055–63

LO, FOR I to myself am unknown, now in God's name
   what must I do?
I adore not the cross nor the crescent, I am not a
   Giaour nor a Jew.
Neither East nor West, land nor sea, is my home; I
   have kin not with angel nor gnome;
I am wrought not of fire nor of foam, I am shaped not
   of dust nor of dew.
I was born not in China afar, not in Saqsin and not in
   Bulghar;
Not in India, where five rivers are, not Iraq nor
   Khurasan I grew.
Not in this world nor that world I dwell, not in
   paradise, neither in hell;
Not from Eden and Rizwan I fell, not from Adam my
   lineage I drew.
In a place beyond uttermost place, in a tract without
   shadow or trace,
Soul and body transcending, I live in the soul of my
   loved one anew!

DIVAN-I SHAMS 31

HUMAN BEINGS climb the ladder of egotism, but in the
end everyone must fall from this ladder.
The higher you climb, the more foolish you are, for
your bones will be more badly broken.
When you die to yourself and come alive through God,
in truth you have become one with God, in absolute
unity.

MASNAVI IV:2763–7

THE SPIRITUAL WORLD

The more awake one is to the material world,
the more one is asleep to the spiritual world.
Such material wakefulness is worse than sleep,
since when our soul is not awake to God,
our wakefulness closes the door to divine bounty.

THE MIRROR OF THE DIVINE

E VERY ROSE that is sweet-scented is telling of the secrets of the Universal.

MASNAVI I:2022

IT WAS a fair orchard, full of trees and fruit
And vines and greenery. A Sufi there
Sat with eyes closed, his head upon his knee,
Sunk deep in mystical meditation.
"Why," asked another, "do you not behold
These signs of God the Merciful displayed
Around you, which He bids us contemplate?"
"The signs," he answered, "I behold within;
Without is nothing but symbols of the signs."

What is all beauty in the world? The image,
Like quivering boughs reflected in a stream,
Of that eternal Orchard which abides
Unwithered in human hearts.

MASNAVI IV:1358–65

THE LOVER'S ailment is not like any other;
Love is the astrolabe of God's mysteries.
Whether love is from earth or heaven,
It leads to God.

MASNAVI I:110–11

THOSE WHO deny God are like a man who, forsaking the beauty of sunshine and moonlight, has buried his head in a pit, only to ask, "If the spirit of God is present in nature, then where is its light?" In order to see the beauty of God around him, he must first lift up his head and look.

MASNAVI III:4796–7

THE HANDIWORK of God can be seen all around us, but few can see the attributes of God which brought that handiwork into existence.

MASNAVI II:2812

GO TO the workshop where the universe was made, and see the Worker. But since the work has become a veil between you and the Worker, you can only see Him in His work. And since the workshop is His dwelling-place, those on the outside cannot see Him. So enter the workshop – that is, non-existence – and see the work and the Worker together.

MASNAVI II:759–62

HOW COULD the foam-flecked waves move without a current? How could dust rise into the air without wind? Since you have seen the dust – namely the form – perceive the wind. The wind is invisible; we only see its effect on external forms, and it is in external forms that we can see the divine spirit, the wind of God. Dissolve your body in vision and pass into sight, pass into sight, into sight!

MASNAVI VI:1459–60; 1463

THE BEAUTY and grandeur of God belong to Him; the beauty and grandeur of the world of creation are borrowed from Him.

MASNAVI II:1103

KNOW THAT the world of created beings is like pure and clear water, reflecting the attributes of God. Their knowledge, justice and kindness reflects God's like a heavenly star is reflected in running water. Earthly kings reflect God's kingship. Scholars mirror the wisdom of God. People and nations may change as one generation replaces another; but the divine attributes are eternal. The water flowing in the stream changes many times, but the reflection of the moon and stars in the water remains the same.

MASNAVI VI:3172–8

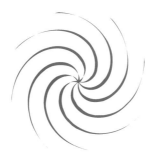

THE EXTERNAL form of the earth is made of dust, but internally it consists of light. The external appearance is at war with the internal reality – as if the shell were at war with the pearl it contains. The external says, "I am this and no more." The internal says, "Look closely, and you will find me." The external says, "The inner reality is an illusion." The internal says, "Wait and see. I shall reveal the truth."

MASNAVI IV:1007–10

THE HUMAN SPIRIT

THE BODY is visible, the spirit concealed. The body is like the sleeve, the spirit the arm within it. The intellect is also hidden but one can perceive both the intellect and the spirit in a person's behavior.

MASNAVI II:3253–4

THE HUMAN spirit is hidden, unknowable. Through our words and actions we reveal the inner nature of its spiritual substance. The essence of this spirit is unchanging, but its expression – our words and actions – is fleeting and subject to change. Our prayer, spiritual battles, and fasting are all transient, but the spirit that gave rise to them remains for ever. Our human spirit rubbed its substance on the touchstone of divine command.

MASNAVI V:246–50

THE BODY is a tent for the spirit,
An ark for Noah.

MASNAVI II:455

THE HUMAN spirit is luminous, and seeks out that which is good. The ego is dark and influenced by the senses. So how does the ego vanquish the spirit? It prevails because the home of the ego is the body, while the spirit is a stranger in this physical world. The dog defends its own territory like a fierce lion.

MASNAVI III:2557–8

THE HUMAN condition is like this: an angel's wing was brought and tied to a donkey's tail so that the donkey perchance might take on the qualities of the angel, whose radiance falls on it.

FIHI MA FIHI 26

WHEN THE time comes for the embryo to receive the
   spirit of life, the sun becomes its helper.
This embryo is brought to life, for the sun endows it
   with spirit.
From the other stars this embryo received only an
   impression, until the sun shone upon it.
How did it become connected with the shining sun in
   the womb?
The sun has many ways, hidden from our senses: the
   way whereby gold is enriched, the way a common
   stone becomes a garnet and the ruby red, the way
   fruit is ripened and the way courage is gifted to one
   distraught with fear.

MASNAVI I:3775–82

THE SUN, which is spirit, became separated into rays by
the windows, which are bodies.
When you gaze on the sun's disk, it is one, but
whoever is screened by his perception of bodies is
in some doubt.
Plurality is in the animal spirit; the human spirit is
one essence.
Inasmuch as God sprinkled His light upon humanity,
human beings are essentially one.
In reality, His light never separated.

MASNAVI II:186–9

THE SPIRIT is like a falcon,
The body its fetter.
Poor, foot-bound, broken-winged creature!

MASNAVI V:2280

THE CORE of every fruit
  is better than its rind.
Regard the body as the rind,
  and the human spirit the core.

MASNAVI III:3417

YOU WHO are in love with your intellect – considering
yourself superior to worshipers of form – that intellect is
but a beam of Universal Intellect cast upon your senses;
regard it as a gilding of gold upon your copper.

MASNAVI II:710–11

THE INTELLECT has two forms. The first is acquired, learned from books and teachers, by reflection and memorizing, through logic and the sciences. In this way your intellectual powers increase, but the more knowledge you acquire, the more you are burdened. The second form of intellect is a gift from God. Its fountainhead is the very heart of the human soul. When the water of divine knowledge bubbles up from the spirit into the intellect, it is clear and sparkling and can never become stagnant or dull.

MASNAVI IV:1960–5

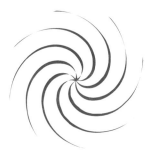

THE HUMAN spirit is in reality awareness that has been honed by tests and trials. Those who have greater awareness have greater spirits. The human spirit is greater than the animal spirit, because it has greater awareness. In turn, the angel spirit is greater than the human spirit because it transcends our level of awareness while the spirit of a saint is greater than that of angels. Those who have less awareness should learn at the feet of those who have greater awareness. A rose does not bow down in worship to a thorn.

MASNAVI II:3326–32

YOUR PHYSICAL attributes, like your body, are merely borrowed. Do not set your heart on them, for they are transient and only last for an hour. Your spirit by contrast is eternal: your body is on this earth, like a lamp, but its light comes from that everlasting Source above.

MASNAVI IV:1840–2

THE PURPOSE OF LIFE

GOD HAS placed a ladder before our feet: we must climb
    it, step by step.
You have feet: why pretend to be lame? You have
    hands: why conceal the fingers that grip? . . .
If you bear God's burden, He will raise you up.
If you accept His commands, He will shower you with
    His grace and bounty.
If you seek union with Him, you will become united
    for evermore.

MASNAVI I:929–31; 936–7

IT WAS our Creator who led us through the stages of evolution, from the animal state to the human. His purpose was to make us intelligent and aware, so that we might know Him.

MASNAVI IV:3646–7

THE WORLD is like a courtroom, with God as our judge. We are called upon to fulfill our covenant with God, who asked, "Am I not your Lord?" To which we answered, "Yea." And since here on earth we are on trial, our every word and action form the witnesses to and the evidence of that agreement.

MASNAVI V:174–6

DO NOT strive so much to achieve your worldly
ambitions; strive only in your religious affairs.
Otherwise at the end your life will be unfulfilled, your
bread unbaked.
Your sepulchre is not beautified by means of stone,
wood, and plaster;
But by digging for yourself a grave of spiritual purity
and burying yourself in His Self,
And by becoming His dust and immersing yourself in the
love of God, so that His breath fills and inspires you.
A tomb adorned with domes and turrets is not
desirable to the followers of truth.
Look at a man decked in satin – how does his lavish
dress help his understanding at all?
His soul writhes in torment, the scorpion of anguish
embedded in his grief-stricken heart.
His physical appearance is embellished with
embroidery and decorations, but inside he is
moaning, consumed with bitter thoughts,
While another passes, his cloak old and patched, but
his thoughts are as sweet as the sugar-cane, his
words like honey!

MASNAVI III:128–37

OUR WORDS and actions testify to our hidden thoughts;
together they express our inner spirit. This is our life's
testimony, our purpose here on earth: to manifest the
very nature of our spirit, which is touched by the spirit of God.

MASNAVI V:236; 250

LITTLE BY little God takes away human beauty:
    little by little the sapling withers.
Go, recite, "To whomever we give a length of days,
    we also cause them to decline."
Seek the spirit;
    do not set your heart on bones.

MASNAVI II:714–15

THE WORLD is a prison and we are the prisoners:
Dig a hole in the prison wall and let yourself out!

MASNAVI I:982

THE SOUL says to her base earthly parts, "My exile is
    more bitter than yours: I am celestial."
The body desires green herbs and running water,
    because its origin is from those;
The soul desires life and the Living One, because its
    origin is the Infinite Soul.
The desire of the soul is for knowledge and wisdom;
    the desire of the body is for orchards, meadows, and
    vines.
The desire of the soul is for ascent and sublimity; the
    desire of the body is for gain and means of self-
    indulgence.

MASNAVI III:4435–9

DO NOT make your home in other men's land;
Do your own work, not the work of a stranger.
Who is the stranger?
Your earthly body, the source of all your sorrow.

MASNAVI II:263–4

EVEN THOUGH in the world you are the most learned
    scholar of the time,
Behold the vanishing of this world and this time!

MASNAVI I:2845

YOU HAVE learned a trade in order to earn a living to satisfy
the needs of your body: now focus on learning your
spiritual trade so that you can look after the needs of your
soul. Here in this world you have become rich and wear
expensive clothes: when you leave this world, how will you fare?

Devote yourself to that spiritual work whose wages are God's
forgiveness in the world beyond. It is a city full of barter and
wages, but do not imagine that your earnings here will be
sufficient. God has said that they are child's play compared to
the earnings in the next world.

It is the same when children play at setting up shop: their
goods and play money are only of use in their game; they are of
no value in the real world. This world is like a playground, and
death is night, when you return home with an empty purse,
tired out. The wages of religion are love, inner rapture, and
nearness to God.

MASNAVI II:2592–6; 600–1

The Purpose of Life ❧ 65

A MAN'S head may be filled with knowledge of meaningless worldly matters, he may be familiar with all the sciences, and yet not know his own soul. He knows the special properties of every substance, but he is as ignorant as an ass about the nature of his own essence. He declares, "I know what is permissible and what is not," but he does not know if his own actions are permissible. He knows the precise value of every article he buys and sells; but in his folly he does not know his own value. He has learned to distinguish auspicious stars from inauspicious ones, but he does not examine his soul to see if he is in a fortunate or poor spiritual state. To know yourself, and to live your life in anticipation of the Day of Judgment, is to master the highest science.

MASNAVI III:2648–54

WHY ARE you surprised that a human spirit cannot remember where it came from, where it came into being and resided before it was born? In this dream-like world, the human spirit is shrouded by a veil as clouds block out the stars, so it can no longer see its former spiritual abode. The task of the human spirit on earth is to purify its heart to enable it to see through the veil and focus on the spiritual realm. The heart must pierce the mystery of this life and see the beginning and the end with unclouded vision.

MASNAVI IV:3632–6

The Purpose of Life ✦ 67

O YOU, who have made it easy for us to labor fruitlessly
    and without reward in this world,
Deliver us!
To us it seems a tempting bait, but it is really a hook:
Show it to us as it really is.

MASNAVI II:466–7

THE BEGINNING, which is thought,
    finds its end in action.
The fruits are first in our thoughts,
    but only in the end are they truly seen.
When you have done the work
    and planted the tree,
When the fruit appears,
    you read the first words.

MASNAVI II:970–2

GOD'S PURPOSE for man is to acquire a seeing eye and an understanding heart.

DIVAN-I SHAMS 10906

EVERYTHING, EXCEPT love of the most beauteous God, even though outwardly it seems as pleasant as eating sweets, is in reality an agony of spirit. What is meant by agony of spirit? It is to advance toward physical death without drinking the Water of Life.

MASNAVI I:3686–7

A LIFE BEYOND

DO NOT cry, "Alas, you are gone!" at my graveside:
For me, this is a time of joyful meeting!
Do not bid me, "Farewell" when I am lowered into my
    grave:
I have passed through the curtain to eternal grace!

DIVAN-I SHAMS 911

EVERYONE IS so frightened of death,
But the true Sufis just laugh;
Nothing overpowers their hearts.
What strikes the oyster shell
Does not harm the pearl.

MASNAVI I:3495–6

IF THE spiritual universe and the way to it were shown,
No one would remain in this world for a single moment.

MASNAVI I:2101

WHEN I die and you wish to visit me,
Do not come to my grave without a drum,
For at God's banquet mourners have no place.

DIVAN-I SHAMS 683

THIS WORLD is like a dream, but you, the sleeper,
    imagine it is real,
Until suddenly death dawns and you will be released
    from the night of opinion and falsehood.
You will laugh at the sorrows that beset your earthly
    existence when you see your permanent dwelling-
    place.
On waking you will become aware of everything you
    did in your sleep in this earthbound existence.
Do not imagine that your deeds will be regarded
    merely as evil actions committed while asleep, with
    no consequences for you.
But in the hour of awakening your tears of grief and
    wails of lamentation will turn to joy!

MASNAVI IV:3654–61

THE SOIL is faithful to its trust:
Whatever you have sown in it, you reap the same.
But until springtime brings the token of God,
The soil does not reveal its secrets.

MASNAVI I:509; 511

THE BODY, like a mother, is pregnant with the spirit-child: death is the pangs and throes of giving birth. All the spirits who have passed on to the next life are waiting anxiously to see how that proud spirit will be born.

MASNAVI I:3514–15

GOD GAVE you life and bestowed on you His attributes; eventually you will return to Him.

MASNAVI III:4182

DEATH IS in reality spiritual birth, the release of the spirit from the prison of the senses into the freedom of God, just as physical birth is the release of the baby from the prison of the womb into the freedom of the world. While childbirth causes pain and suffering to the mother, for the baby it brings liberation.

MASNAVI III:3556–60

THOSE TO whom death seems as sweet as sugar,
How can their sight be dazzled by the temptations of
    this earthly realm?
Physical death holds no bitterness for them,
They see it as a blessed refuge from a prison cell into a
    glorious garden.
It will deliver them from a world of torment:
No one weeps for the loss of such nothingness!
If an earthquake brings the walls of the prison
    crashing down,
Will the heart of any prisoner be downcast?
Will they complain, "Alas, this marble stone is broken,
And our spirits and souls have escaped confinement.
We admired the quality and beauty of the marble and
    stone of our prison.
Why did the earthquake destroy it, allowing the
    prisoners to escape?"
No prisoner would talk such nonsense, unless the
    gallows was his final destination after prison.
Death cannot have a bitter taste to the person who is
    given sugar in exchange for snake poison.
The soul, freed from the turmoil and limitations of the
    body on death, soars on wings of the spirit,

Like the prisoner in his cell who falls asleep at night
    and dreams of a beautiful rose-garden,
And says, "O God, do not make me return to my body,
    but allow me to wander like a prince in this
    garden."
God replies, "I will grant your prayer; you may stay."
Think how delightful such a dream must be!
Without dying, the dreamer finds himself in paradise.
Does he feel any regret for his former waking life or for
    the body still in chains in the prison cell?
If you are a true believer, arise now, enter the ranks of
    battle, for a feast has been prepared for you in
    heaven.
Close your lips against food and drink: hasten toward
    the heavenly table.
Keep your gaze steadfastly fixed on heaven, quivering
    like the willow in your desire to attain it.

MASNAVI V:1712–27; 1730–1

A MAN once said, "This world would be delightful, were it not for the threat of death."

His friend answered, "Without death, this complex world would not be worth a fig.

It would be like a corn-stick in the field, left unthreshed and neglected, the corn uneaten.

You have confused what is really death with life, but you have sown your seed in barren soil."

O God, show us everything as it really is in this house of illusion.

No one who has died is sad as a result: his grief is due to the realization that he has not set by enough provisions for the life hereafter.

Otherwise he would be happy, because he has left a prison and finds himself in open fields, filled with delight.

From this place of mourning and dungeon of suffering he has been transported to a spacious plain,

A "seat of truth," instead of a palace of falsehood, a choice wine instead of buttermilk.

And God is there beside him: he is delivered from the
    material world and all its afflictions.
And if you have not yet taken up the spiritual path, one
    or two moments remain: die to the self!

MASNAVI V:1760–71

I DIED to the mineral state and became a plant,
I died to the plant and rose to animal,
I died from animality and became human,
Why then should I fear death?
When have I become less by dying?
At the next stage I will die only to be transformed,
To soar on high among the angels.
But even from angelhood I will pass on:
"Everything perishes except God."
Once more I will sacrifice my angel state
To become at last what you could never imagine:
I shall become non-existence!
"Verily, unto Him we shall return."

MASNAVI III:3901–6

IF ANYONE were to tell a baby in the womb: "Outside is an
   ordered world,
A pleasant earth, wide and open, brimming with
   thousands of delights and many things to eat;
Mountains and seas and plains, fragrant orchards,
   gardens and fertile fields,
A lofty sky alight with sunshine, moonbeams and
   innumerable stars;
Its wonders are beyond description: why do you stay,
   drinking blood, in this cramped cell of filth and pain?" –
The baby, being what it is, would turn away in utter
   disbelief, for the blind have no imagination.
It has never experienced anything beyond the womb,
   and cannot visualize such a place.
So, in this world, when the saints tell of a world beyond,
   without scent or color,
Nobody listens to them: attachment to this physical
   world is a huge barrier,
Just as the baby's craving for the blood that nourishes it
   in its mother's womb
Prevented it from perceiving the external world, since it
   knows no food but blood.

MASNAVI III:53–68

O F ALL the different types of knowledge, on the day of death the best preparation and provision for your journey is the knowledge of spiritual poverty.

MASNAVI I:2834

WHAT DO you really possess,
And what have you gained in this life?
What pearls have you brought up
From the depths of the sea?
On the day of death,
Your physical senses will vanish.
Do you have the spiritual light
To illumine your heart?
When dust fills your eyes in the grave,
Will your grave shine brightly?

MASNAVI II:939–41

A CERTAIN MAN came to a goldsmith. "Give me the scales," he said, "so that I may weigh some gold."

"Go away," said the goldsmith. "I do not have a sieve."

"Give me the scales," the man repeated, "and have done with such jokes."

"I have no broom in the shop," replied the goldsmith.

"Enough, enough!" said the man. "No more of these jests. Give me the scales I am asking for. Do not pretend to be deaf and stop talking in riddles."

"I heard what you said," responded the goldsmith. "I am not deaf, nor am I in my dotage. I know what you asked for, but you are a trembling old man. Your hand shakes, that gold of yours consists of the tiniest filings, and so the fragments of gold will spill. Then you will say, 'Bring me a broom, so that I may search for my gold in the dust.' And when you have swept it up you will find dust mixed with your gold, and then you will ask for a sieve.' I saw the end completely from the beginning. Go away, and good day to you!"

From the beginning of the enterprise, discern the end, that you may not repent on the Day of Judgment.

MASNAVI III:1624–33

THE SUFI
WAY

The Sufi's book is not of ink and letters;
it is nothing but a heart as white as snow.

TRANSCENDING THE SELF

ONE MORNING a woman asked her lover, as a test, "Do you love me more than you love yourself?" He replied, "I love you so much that I am full of you from head to toe. There is nothing left of my own existence except my name." If you love God, you will feel toward Him as that lover felt toward his beloved.

MASNAVI V:2020–4

THIS SELF of ours is a part of hell.
Only with the power of God can one overcome it.

MASNAVI I:1382–3

THE CHAMPION who breaks the enemy's ranks is of little account compared to the true victor who overcomes his own self.

MASNAVI I:1389

THE INTELLIGENT desire self-control;
Children want sweets.

MASNAVI I:1601–2

AS FAR as you can, become a slave, not a monarch.
Endure blows: be the ball and not the bat.

MASNAVI I:1868

EVERYONE IS a child
  except the one who is intoxicated with God.
No one is an adult
  except the one who is free from desire.

MASNAVI I:3430

WHAT IS the mirror of Being? Non-being.
Bring non-being as your gift, if you are not a fool.

MASNAVI I:3201

YOU ARE a shadow: annihilate
  yourself in the rays of the Sun!
How long will you look at your shadow?
  Look also at His light!

DIVAN-I SHAMS 20395

MY EGO passed away
    for the sake of God's ego,
And He remained alone;
    I roll at His feet like dust.
The individual self can become dust,
    in which only His footprints remain.
Become dust at His feet
    for the sake of His footprints,
     and one day you will be His crown.

MASNAVI II:1173–6

IT SUITS the generous man to give money,
    but the generosity of the lover lies in the surrender
    of his soul.
If you give bread for God's sake,
    you will be given bread in return.
If you give your life for God's sake,
    you will be given life in return.

MASNAVI I:2235–6

YOU ARE a lover of God and when God comes to you, not a single hair on your head will remain. At a glance from God, hundreds like you will be reduced to nothing, your egos consumed in the love of God. You are like a shadow, in love with the sun; in the presence of the sun the shadow swiftly vanishes.

MASNAVI III:4621–3

WHEN A candle burns in full sunlight, the flame of the candle is so overwhelmed by the brightness of the sun that it is barely visible. The flame does not cease to exist, but its light is consumed by the sunshine. Similarly, when a person's spirit comes near to God, it is overwhelmed by the spirit of God. The individual spirit continues to exist; but its attributes have been wholly absorbed into God's attributes.

MASNAVI III:3669–73

YOU HAVE suffered agonies
    but you are still far from God,
Because you have not fulfilled
    your purpose of dying to the self.
Your agonies will not cease
    until you die.

You cannot reach the roof
    unless you climb the ladder.
When two rungs are missing
    you will be unable to climb,
When the bucket's rope is too short
    it will not reach the water in the well.

MASNAVI VI:723–6

IF YOU join the ranks of those who ascend from the level
   of the human spirit,
The steed of not-being, or self-annihilation, will carry
   you aloft like Buraq.
It will not be like the ascension of a mortal to the moon,
   but rather like the ascension of a sugar-cane to sugar.
It will not be like the ascension of vapor to the sky,
   but like the ascension of an embryo to rationality.
The steed of selflessness, if you are truly non-existent,
   brings you to real existence.

MASNAVI IV:552–5

KILL THE cow of your ego as quickly as you can, so that your inner spirit can come to life and attain true awareness.

MASNAVI II:1446

To BECOME spiritual, you must die to self, and come alive in the Lord. Only then will the mysteries of God fall from your lips. To die to self through self-discipline causes suffering but brings you everlasting life.

MASNAVI III:3364–5

NOTHING CAN guide you except a power that preserves
    the spirit of the devout from the keepers of the
    shooting stars.
No one can enter the audience chamber of divine
    majesty until he becomes selfless.
How can we ascend to heaven? Through selflessness,
    the creed and religion of the lovers of God.

MASNAVI VI:231–3

PURIFY YOURSELF from the attributes of self, so that you may see your own pure, untarnished essence.

MASNAVI I:3460

YOUR SELF is the mother of all idols: the material idol is only a snake, but the spiritual idol of the self is a dragon.

It is easy to break a material idol, very easy; to regard the self as easy to subdue is only folly.

O son, if you wish to know the form of the self, read the description of hell with its seven gates.

At every moment the self issues an act of deceit; and in each of those deceits a hundred Pharaohs and their followers are drowned.

MASNAVI I:772; 778–80

O PEACOCK, do not tear out your feathers, but detach
   your heart from pride in them: the existence of a
   foe is indispensable for waging this holy war.
When there is no enemy, you cannot fight your
   spiritual battle: if you did not feel lust, you could
   not obey God's command.
There cannot be self-restraint without desire: when
   there is no adversary, what need for courage?
Hark, do not castrate yourself, do not become a monk:
   chastity depends on the existence of lust.
Without suffering the pain of self-restraint, no
   recompense can follow.
How admirable is that conditional bond, and how
   uplifting the recompense, a recompense that
   charms the heart and increases the life of the spirit!

MASNAVI V:574–7; 584–5

WHATEVER INSTRUMENT God makes of me, I become.
If He makes me a cup, I become a cup;
If He makes me a dagger, I become a dagger.
If He makes me a fountain, then I shall give water;
If He makes me fire, then I shall give heat.
If He makes me rain, I shall bring forth the harvest;
If He makes me an arrow, I shall pierce the body.
If He makes me a snake, I shall produce poison;
If He makes me His friend, I shall serve Him well.
I am like a pen in His hand which he moves as He
    wills.

MASNAVI V:1685–90

PURIFYING THE HEART

THE PURE heart is a spotless mirror in which images of infinite beauty are reflected. Moses, that perfect saint, reflected in the mirror of his heart the infinite form of the One who is formless, the image of the One who is unseen. This form, this image, cannot be contained in heaven, nor in the ocean, nor in the universe. All these have limits, but the mirror of the heart has no limit.

MASNAVI I:3485–8

THE CHINESE said to the sultan, "We are the better artists," and the Greeks rejoined, "We have greater skill and aesthetic sense." The sultan decided to set them a challenge to settle the matter, and gave each a room, with a curtain separating them.

The Chinese asked the sultan for a hundred different colors, gold and silver, and gems. The Greeks asked only for polish and polishing cloths and shut themselves in their room and polished industriously.

When the Chinese finished their work, the sultan entered and looked at the pictures they had painted. He was awed by the sight. Then the Greeks raised the curtain that separated the rooms. The reflection of the Chinese paintings fell on their polished walls, and all that the sultan had seen before seemed even more beautiful there.

The Greeks are the Sufis who, without formal learning, have purified their hearts from every trace of greed, lust, envy, and hatred.

MASNAVI I:3467–84

WHEN THE mirror of your heart becomes clear and pure,
You will behold images from beyond this realm of
    earth and water.
You will see both the images and the image-Maker,
Both the carpet of spiritual existence
And the carpet-Spreader.

MASNAVI II:72–3

SUFIS ARE a mirror for the soul – better than a mirror,
For they have polished their hearts in remembrance of
    God and meditation,
Until their heart's mirror reflects a true image of the
    Original.

MASNAVI I:3153–4

IN THE limitlessness of the pure heart
   understanding leads to silence,
   because that heart is with God
   or indeed it is He.
Those with mirror-like hearts
   have left behind mere fragrance and color:
   each moment they behold beauty without
   hindrance.
They have discarded the outer form
   and raised the banner
   of mystical intuition.
Thought is gone, all is light.
They have reached the essence
   and the Ultimate Source of knowledge.

MASNAVI I:3489–94

IF THE heart is restored to health, and purged of sensuality, then "the Merciful God is seated on His Throne." After this, He guides the heart directly, since the heart is with Him.

MASNAVI I:3665–6

DO NOT put musk on your body:
Rub it on your heart.
What is musk?
The holy name of the glorious God.
The hypocrite puts musk on his body
And puts his spirit in the ash-pit.

MASNAVI II:267–8

EVERYONE SEES the inner reality of things, and even the future, according to her insight and spiritual enlightenment. This in turn increases in proportion to the purity of her heart. The more she polishes her heart's mirror, the more she can see in it, and the more the hidden mysteries are revealed to her. That spiritual purity is given to us by the grace of God, and our success in polishing our hearts is also a divine bounty.

MASNAVI IV:2902; 2909–11

WATER LEAKING into the boat is the ruin of the boat,
But water under the boat is its support.
Since Solomon cast out the desire for wealth and
    possessions from his heart,
He did not call himself by any name but "poor."
The stoppered jar, though in rough water,
Floated because of its empty heart.
When the wind of poverty is in anyone,
He floats peacefully on the surface of the water of this
    world.

MASNAVI I:985–8

O GOD, make our stony hearts as soft as wax;
Make our wailing sweet to Your ears and the object of
    Your mercy.

MASNAVI II:1992

THE MIRROR of the heart must be clear,
So you can discern the ugly from the beautiful.

MASNAVI II:2063

I F YOU are enraged by every blow, how will your mirror be
polished? How will your heart become pure?

MASNAVI I:2980

IF YOUR thought is a rose,
    you are a rose garden;
And if it is a thorn,
    you are fuel for the fire.

MASNAVI II:278

THE BEAUTY of the heart is the lasting beauty: its lips give to drink of the water of life. Truly it is the water, the giver of drink, and the one who drinks: all three become one when your talisman is shattered. That oneness cannot be grasped by reasoning.

MASNAVI II:716–18

THE HEART is purified by godliness.
If the mirror of the heart is encrusted,
   much polishing is required until it is at last spotless.
If the mirror is very fine, like a fertile seed-bed,
   only a little polish is needed.

MASNAVI V:456–8

FREE WILL

GOD'S FREE will has given rise to our own free will. His free will is invisible beneath the dust; it creates our free will. His commands to us acknowledge our free will: He does not compel obedience, but invites it.

MASNAVI V:3087–8

WITHOUT DOUBT human beings have free will: look at the evidence around us.

No one orders a stone, "Come here!" nor would you expect that inanimate object to respond.

Similarly no one tells a person to fly, or a blind man to see.

No one says to a stone, "You are late," or to a stick, "Why did you strike that blow?"

Nor would you say such things to a person who has no free will, and only acts under compulsion.

Obligations and prohibitions, honor and rebuke only concern those who possess free will.

MASNAVI V:2967–73

HUMAN BEINGS have free will in the matter of injustice and wrong-doing.

This free will is rooted in our inner spirit, in our hearts.

MASNAVI V:2974–5

HERE IS a parable to illustrate the difference between compulsion and free will: when someone is frightened, his hands might tremble, which is an involuntary physical reaction. He may also hit another person. God has made both these movements possible, but you cannot compare them. You may regret striking someone, but no one feels sorry for something that was involuntary.

MASNAVI I:1496–9

FREE WILL is the salt of our devotion to God, otherwise there would be no merit in it. The earth revolves involuntarily, and its movement deserves neither reward nor punishment. Only actions undertaken as a result of our free will may be weighed on the Day of Judgment.

MASNAVI III:3287–8

YOUR FREE will, your power to choose good or evil, is increased by the inspirations of the angel and the promptings of the devil. The angel and the devil, presenting opposing choices to us, force us to exercise our free will, which is a faculty within us.

MASNAVI V:2985; 3004–5

FREE WILL is the endeavor to thank God for His beneficence; predestination is the denial of that beneficence.

MASNAVI I:938

THE SPIRITUALLY enlightened choose freely to devote themselves to the work of the next world; the foolish choose freely the work of this.

MASNAVI I:638

"ON ACCOUNT of my gorgeous plumage I suffer hundreds of afflictions," complained the peacock. "Fowlers lay traps for me and hunters shoot at me, all for the sake of my feathers. Since I have neither the strength nor self-control to protect myself, it would be better if I were to pluck them out. They tempt my pride."

Human talents and accomplishments can lead to the downfall of the spiritually weak. Free will only leads to good when exercised by someone who has self-control and who fears God. With self-control and moral safeguards, the spiritual strengths of such a person increase when he exercises his free will. In the absence of these, he should abandon free will before it leads him into sin.

MASNAVI V:642–55

A SEEING EYE

FREEDOM FROM prejudice gives discernment and light to
the eyes, while self-interest blinds you and
prejudice buries your knowledge in a grave.
Lack of prejudice makes ignorance wise;
prejudice makes knowledge perverse.
Withstand temptation, and your sight is clear;
act selfishly, and you become blind and enslaved.

MASNAVI II:2750–3

ALTHOUGH THESE shells of bodies in the world
    are all living by grace of the Sea of the Soul –
    there is not a pearl in every shell.
Open your eyes and look
    into the heart of each one.
Find out what is within each one,
    for that costly pearl is rarely found.

MASNAVI II:1023–5

WHEN THE ear is penetrating, it becomes an eye.
Otherwise, the word of God becomes enmeshed in the
    ear and does not reach the heart.

MASNAVI II:862

A SEEING eye is better than three hundred blind men's
    sticks:
The eye can distinguish pearls from pebbles.

MASNAVI VI:3785

THE LAMPS are different, but the light is the same: it comes
  from beyond.

If you look at the lamp, you will be lost: for from this arises
  the appearance of number and plurality.

Focus on the light, and you will see beyond the dualism
  inherent in the finite body.

O you who are the kernel of existence, the disagreement
  between Muslim, Zoroastrian and Jew depends on this
  perspective:

Some Hindus had brought an elephant for exhibition and
placed it in a dark room. Crowds of people were going into that
dark place to see it. Finding that their eyes could not penetrate
the darkness, each felt it with his palm.

The palm of one fell on the trunk.

"This creature is like a water-spout," he said.

The hand of another lighted on the elephant's ear. To him
the beast was evidently like a fan.

Another ran his hand down its leg.

"To me the elephant's shape is like a pillar," he said.

Another laid his hand on its back.

"Certainly this elephant is like a throne," he said.

Depending on their different viewpoints, their descriptions varied. Had each held a candle, these differences would have disappeared. The sensual eye is just like the palm of the hand. The palm cannot cover the whole of the animal.

The eye of the Sea is one thing and the foam another. Let the foam, the object itself, go, and gaze with the eye of the Sea, the eye of Reality. Day and night foam-flecks are flung from the sea. O amazing! You focus on the foam but not the sea.

MASNAVI III:1259–71

IF A saint wears a veil of madness,
Will you who are blind recognize him?
But, if your inner eye is open,
Behold a spiritual giant under every stone.
To the eye that is open,
Every dervish cloak conceals
A Moses in its folds.

MASNAVI II:2346–8

SINCE YOUR vision is so limited,
Close your eyes and see with the eyes of God.
His sight for ours – what a recompense!
With His divine perception,
You will find everything you desire.

MASNAVI I:921–2

THE EYE is given sight through nearness to God.

MASNAVI II:2309

EVERYONE, ACCORDING to their spiritual enlightenment,
and in proportion to the polishing of their heart's
mirror, sees the hidden meaning of things.
The more you polish your heart, the more you see
with your inner eye.

MASNAVI IV:2909–10

OUTER, PHYSICAL light comes from the sun, while inner
light comes from the reflection of the rays of divine
glory.
The light which shines in the eye is really the light of
the heart, while the light which infuses the heart is
the light of God, which is pure and unconnected to
the light of intellect and sense.

MASNAVI I:1125–7

EVERYONE IS aware of God's mercy, and everyone is aware of his worth. Everyone flees from His wrath, and clings to his mercy. But God has hidden wrath in His mercy, and hidden mercy in His wrath. This is God's mystery and wisdom. In this way people of discernment, who see by the light of God, may be distinguished from those who see only the immediate, outer form of things.

MASNAVI V:419FF

THOUGH THE master was very generous,
Yet it could not compare, Lord, with Your bounty.
He gave the hat, but You the head with reason,
He gave the coat, You gave the tall physique.
He gave me gold, but You the hand to count it,
He gave a mule, You the mind to ride it.
The master gave me a candle, but You the eyesight.
He gave me wages, You life and existence,
He promised riches, but You the purity of spirit.

MASNAVI VI:3125–9

DISCERNMENT FLIES
  from one who is drunk with empty desire.
He who puts away that cup
  illumines his inner eye,
    and the hidden is revealed.

M OST PEOPLE are unable to perceive the essence of the attributes of divine perfection. Nothing in existence is as mysterious as the essence and consciousness of God. His attributes are mysteries; the essences of these attributes are mysteries of mysteries. Those who attain perfection are able to penetrate these mysteries, and so understand the essence of God Himself. They are true lovers of God, and nothing is hidden from them.

MASNAVI III:3650–3

WHEN HAVE you done something wrong
    without suffering the consequences?
When have you done something good
    without blessings being showered upon you?

If you grasp the cord of understanding
    and look at this world with a seeing eye,
You will not need to wait till Judgment Day
    to see the effects of all your actions.
If you want a pure heart, be observant,
    and see for every act its own response.

MASNAVI IV:2458–61; 2467

LIVING IN THE SPIRIT

Union with God will turn your thorns into roses.

A LIFE OF FAITH

THE REWARDS of a life of faith and devotion to God are love and inner rapture, and the capacity to receive the light of God.

MASNAVI II:2601

WHEN YOU put a cargo on board a ship, you make that
    venture on trust,
For you do not know whether you will be drowned or
    safely reach the other shore.
If you say, "I will not embark till I am certain of my
    fate," then you will do no trade: the secret of these
    two destinies is never disclosed.
The faint-hearted merchant neither gains nor loses;
    nay he loses, for he is deprived of his fortune.
Only those who are zealous in their search, who
    faithfully seek the flame, find the light.
Since all affairs turn upon hope, surely faith is the
    worthiest object of hope, for thereby you win
    salvation.

MASNAVI III:3083–91

THE MELODIES of David were so dear to the faithful,
But to the disbeliever they were no more than the
    sawing of wood.

MASNAVI II:1074

A Life of Faith ⤳ 117

REFRESH YOUR faith, but not with talking.
You have secretly refreshed your desires.
As long as desires are fresh, faith is not,
for it is desire that locks that gate.

MASNAVI I:1078–91

THE FAITHFUL believer bows willingly, seeking the good
  pleasure of God and directing his life toward that.
The unbeliever worships God, unwillingly, but he
  directs himself toward some other object of desire.
True, he keeps the King's fortress in good repair, but
  he claims to be in command.
The faithful believer keeps that fortress in good repair
  for the sake of the King, not for status or power.

MASNAVI II:2544–8

THE LIGHT of faith extinguishes the fire of sensuality. On the Day of Judgment, faith will oppose sensuality, since the former was aroused by God's grace, the latter by His wrath. If you wish to overcome the evil of the fire, quench its flames with the waters of divine mercy. The faithful believer is a fountain of that water of mercy: the pure spirit of the well-doer is the Water of Life.

MASNAVI II:1250–3

ALL OPPRESSION has turned into faithfulness,
    all cloudiness to purity!
The attributes of human nature
    have been annihilated,
The attributes of God have come!

DIVAN-I SHAMS 8076

PRAYER AND REMEMBRANCE

OF GOD

I F THE time for prayer had passed, this world would have become a dark place for you, and tears of disappointment and grief would flow like a river from your eyes, because everyone delights in some act of devotion and cannot bear to miss it, even for a short while. That disappointment and grief would have been worth a hundred prayers: what is ritual prayer compared with the glow of humble longing?

MASNAVI II:2769–70

A CERTAIN MAN one night was crying, "God!" till his lips became sweet with the mention of His name.

"Why now, chatterbox," said the Devil, "where is the answer, 'I am here' to all your cries of, 'God?' Not a single answer has come from the throne: how long will you continue to supplicate Him in vain?"

Broken-hearted, the man lay down to sleep. In his dream he heard the divine Voice:

"Your call, 'O God!' is My call, 'I am here.' Your fervent supplication is My message, and all your strivings to reach Me are but My hands at your feet, releasing bonds and drawing you to Me. Your love and fear are the noose to snare My grace! And to your every cry of, 'O my Lord' I answer a hundred times, 'Here I am.' "

MASNAVI III:189–97

I HAVE prayed so much that I have become a living
    prayer –
Everyone who meets me begs a prayer from me.

DIVAN–I SHAMS 903

DRINK THE Word of Wisdom,
    for it is brilliant light
    that God has veiled for you
    as clouds obscure the sun,
        O you whose eyes would weep
        to gaze on the sun's heart.

Drink in this light O soul,
    that soon you may behold
    that pure Light, bright, undimmed,
    that now is hidden.

And soar across the sky,
    radiant as a star –
    no, through the stratosphere,
    unconditioned, heaven-bound,
    beyond earth's gravity
    toward the brilliant Sun.

MASNAVI III:1286–8

NEVER BE without the remembrance of God, for His remembrance provides the bird of the spirit with strength, feathers, and wings.

FIHI MA FIHI 175

PRAYER DOES not consist in forms alone. Formal prayer has a beginning and an end, like all forms and bodies and everything that involves speech and sound, but the soul is unconditioned and infinite: it has neither beginning nor end . . . Prayer is the drowning and unconsciousness of the soul, so that all these forms remain without. At that moment there is no room even for Gabriel, who is pure spirit. A person who prays in this way is exempt from all religious obligations, since he is deprived of his reason. Absorption of the self in divine unity is the soul of prayer.

FIHI MA FIHI 15

THE PURPOSE of ritual prayer is not that you should bow and prostrate yourself all day. Its purpose is that you should develop a prayerful attitude, maintaining the spiritual state obtained in prayer at all times. Whether asleep or awake, at work or rest, you should always remember God: you should be one of those who "are constantly at their prayers."

FIHI MA FIHI 182–3

THESE SAYINGS of mine are really a prayer to God,
  words to lure the breath of that sweet One.
If you seek an answer from God,
  how then can you fail to pray?
How can you be silent, knowing He always replies to
  your, "O Lord?" with, "I am here."
His answer is silent but you can feel it from head to toe.

MASNAVI II: 1189–91

PRAISE AND prayer were given to you, but praying made
your heart proud. You saw yourself as an intimate of God,
but many became distanced from God this way.

MASNAVI II:339–40

IF LOVE were only spiritual,
The practices of fasting and prayer would not exist.
The gifts lovers give each other
Are nothing but outward forms
But they testify to invisible love,
Just as outward acts of kindness
Reveal a loving heart.

MASNAVI I:2625–7

As HE was walking, Moses heard a shepherd praying to God, offering serve Him, to sweep His room, comb His hair, wash His clothes and feet, bring Him food, and kiss His hand. Moses scolded the shepherd for his blasphemy. "God does not need such services from you!" The shepherd tore his clothes in despair and walked into the desert.

That night God appeared to Moses and admonished him. "You have separated My servant from Me. I did not ordain worship for My own benefit, but as a kindness to My servants. Their praise does not glorify Me, but bestows purity and radiance on them. I do not look at their words, but at their spirit and emotions. I gaze into their hearts to see if they are lovely, because the heart is the essence. I want burning, burning! Light up your soul with the fire of love, and burn all thoughts and words away!"

MASNAVI II:1720–63

SEPARATION FROM God is like a well;
Remembrance of Him is the rope.

DIVAN-I SHAMS 19325

BECOME SILENT and in silence move toward non-
   existence,
And when you become non-existent, you will be all
   praise!

DIVAN–I SHAMS 2628

FEED YOUR heart on the love of God that you may become
immortal, and your face illumined with divine light.

MASNAVI II:2442

YOUR BODY of water and clay, when wafted by the
   breath of Jesus,
Spread wings, became a bird, and flew.
Your praise of God is a breath
From your body of water and clay.
It became a bird of paradise
Through the breath of your heart's sincerity.

MASNAVI I:865–7

ACQUIRING VIRTUES

GOD CREATED the physical universe in order to manifest Himself, so that the treasure of His wisdom may be revealed. He said, "I was a hidden treasure." Listen! In the same way you must not let your spiritual reality be submerged, but instead must manifest your spirit in action.

MASNAVI IV:3028–9

COMPANIONSHIP WITH the holy makes you one of them. Though you are rock or marble, you will become a jewel when you associate with the man of heart.

MASNAVI I:721–2

GOD FORBID! I desire nothing from created beings: through contentment there is a whole world within my heart.

MASNAVI I:2362

COURTESY WITHOUT sincerity of the heart and soul
   is like herbs on the ash heap, O friends.
Look at them from a distance and pass by:
   they are not fit to eat or even smell.

MASNAVI II:2840–1

BROKEN PROMISES and agreements are the result of
    stupidity;
Faithfulness to one's word befits one who fears God.

MASNAVI II:2875

I HAVE never seen in this world of trial and probation
Anything more highly prized than a good character.
Whoever has a good temperament and character
    is saved on the Day of Judgment,
While those who are not pure-hearted and virtuous are
    broken.

MASNAVI II:810; 816

NO MIRROR ever became iron again;
No bread ever became wheat;
No ripened grape ever became sour again.
Mature yourself and be secure
From a change for the worse. Become the Light.

MASNAVI II:1317–19

GOD IS as a painter, at work on the pictures of His creation. Every moment He writes what He will on the page of their thought, and then obliterates it. He takes away anger and puts contentment in its place. He takes away stinginess, and puts generosity in its place. Morning and evening this process takes place. You are being filled and emptied, by His hands.

MASNAVI VI:3332–5; 3340

WHAT IS justice? To put something in its correct place. What is injustice? To put something in the wrong place.

MASNAVI VI:2596

VIRTUES AND graces are the signs of a follower of God;
They are the footprints of one who is devoted to Him.

MASNAVI II:1665

Your lower, hellish nature tries to lead you into temptation, but you have struggled hard and now your soul is full of purity. You have quenched the fires of lust for God's sake, and they have been transformed into the light of guidance. The fire of anger has turned to forbearance, the darkness of ignorance to knowledge, the fire of greed to unselfishness, and the thorns of envy to the roses of love.

You have extinguished these fires for the love of God, and converted your fiery nature into a verdant orchard. The nightingales of the remembrance and glorification of God sing sweetly in the garden of your heart. Answering the call of God, you have brought the water of the spirit into the blazing hell of your soul.

MASNAVI II:2560–7

AVOIDING PITFALLS

KNOW THAT every bad habit is a thornbush.
After all, many is the time its thorns have pierced your
feet.

MASNAVI II:1240

THE LION accompanied the hare to the well and looked in. The lion saw his own image reflected in the water, and beside him a plump hare. No sooner did he espy his enemy than he left the hare and sprang into the well. He fell into the pit which he had dug: his aggression recoiled on his own head.

O reader, many of the faults that you see in others are in fact your own reflected in them! In them you see all that you are – your hypocrisy, iniquity, and insolence. It is really your own faults that you are criticizing, but you do not see them as clearly in yourself, or you would hate yourself with all your soul. Like the lion who sprang at his image in the water, you are only hurting yourself, O foolish man. When you reach the bottom of the well of your own nature, then you will know that the wickedness is in you.

As the Prophet said, "The faithful are like mirrors to each other."

MASNAVI I:1304–9; 1319–24; 1328

BEWARE! DO NOT allow yourself to do
What you know is wrong, relying on the thought,
"Later I will repent and ask God's forgiveness."
True repentance flashes remorse and rains tears,
For which lightning and clouds are needed, just as
    warmth and rain are needed to produce fruit.
Without the lightning of the heart and the rain clouds
    of the eyes,
How can the fire of divine wrath be calmed?
How shall the greenery grow
And fountains of clear water pour forth?

MASNAVI II:1652–6

ALONG THE spiritual way there is no harder pass than this:
He is fortunate who does not carry envy as a companion.
Become dust under the feet of the godly, and throw dust
   on the head of envy.

MASNAVI I:431; 436

ANGER AND lust make a man squint;
They cloud the spirit so it strays from truth.
When self-interest appears, virtue hides:
A hundred veils rise up between the heart and the eye.

MASNAVI I:333–4

ANYONE WHO notices his own faults before those of others, would surely be concerned to correct himself. These worldly people do not look at themselves, and so they blame one another.

MASNAVI II:881

WHEN, WITH just a taste,
    envy and deceit arise,
    and ignorance and carelessness are born,
    know you have tasted the unlawful.

MASNAVI I:1645

SUPPRESS YOUR anger: do not let it rise like vomit in
    your throat.
You will receive sweet words in compensation.

MASNAVI I:3379

KNOW THAT a word suddenly shot from the tongue
   is like an arrow shot from the bow.
Son, that arrow will not turn back on its way;
   you must damn a torrent at the source.
O tongue, you are an endless treasure.
O tongue, you are also an endless disease.

MASNAVI I:1658–9;1702

ANYONE NOT flying to the Lord of Glory
   must suppose himself perfect.
There is no worse sickness for the soul,
   O you who are proud, than the conceit of perfection.
The heart and eyes must bleed a lot
   before self-complacency seeps away.

MASNAVI I:3213–15

YOUR WORDS and actions must not contradict each other, so
that your life may be acceptable to God.

MASNAVI V:255

O BROTHER, wisdom is flowing into you
    from the illustrious saint of God,
      but you have only borrowed it.
Although the house of your heart
    is lit up from inside,
      the light-source is a luminous neighbor.
Give thanks; do not be vain or arrogant,
    and pay attention without self-importance.
It is sad that this borrowed state of glory
    has put religious communities
      far from religious communion.

MASNAVI I:3255–8

A CONCEITED person seeing someone sin,
Finds the flames of hell rise up in him.
He calls his hellish pride defense of the religion;
He does not recognize the arrogance of his own soul.

MASNAVI I:3347–8

MANY PEOPLE do works of devotion
   their eyes fixed on approval and reward.
It is really a hidden sin.
That which the pious think pure
   is really foul.

MASNAVI I:3384–5

IN YOUR envy you complain, "I am inferior to so and so. His superiority exaggerates my inferiority." Indeed, envy is a defect; in itself it is worse than any inferiority.

MASNAVI II:804–5

ALITTLE MOUSE once caught a camel's lead-rope in its paws and, emulating a man, began to lead it. Because of the readiness with which the camel set off behind him, the mouse was duped into thinking himself a hero. The flash of his thought struck the camel.

"Go on, enjoy yourself," he grunted. "I will show you!"

Presently the mouse came to the bank of a wide river, and came to an abrupt halt.

"Companion over mountain and plain," said the camel, "why have we stopped? What is the matter? Step forward like a man! Into the river with you! You are my guide and leader; do not halt halfway, paralyzed!"

"But this is a wide and deep river," said the mouse. "I am afraid of drowning, comrade."

"Let me see how deep the water is," said the camel, and quickly set foot in it.

"The water only comes up to my knees," he went on. "Blind mouse, why were you worried? Why did you lose your head?"

"To you it is an ant, but to me it is a dragon," said the mouse. "There are great differences between one knee and another. If it reaches your knee, clever camel, it passes two feet over my head."

"Do not be so arrogant another time," said the camel, "lest you are consumed body and soul by the sparks of my wrath. Emulate mice like yourself; a mouse has no business to hobnob with camels."

"I repent," said the mouse. "For God's sake get me across this deadly water!"

"Listen," said the camel, taking pity on the mouse. "Jump up and sit on my hump. This passage has been entrusted to me; I would take across hundreds of thousands like you."

Since you are not the ruler, be a simple subject; since you are not the captain, do not steer the ship. Since you are not a prophet, follow in their footsteps, which lead from the physical to the spiritual realms. Since you are not the mouthpiece of God, be an ear.

MASNAVI II:3436–56

S O LONG as you are taken in by flattery, O foolish man, your faults and imperfections remain glaring. How will your character be improved by fawning and lies? You store up compliments and praise in your heart like treasure, but in fact the reproaches and criticism of the spiritual would be better for you.

Do not swallow the honey of those who are spiritually lost, but swallow the bile of the spiritual kings, because happiness and honor follow. Under the shelter of the spirit, the body becomes soul.

MASNAVI II:2583–7

HELL IS a dragon with seven heads. Greed is the bait which draws you into its snare.

MASNAVI VI:4657

WHEN SOMEONE criticizes or disagrees with you, a small ant of hatred and antagonism is born in your heart. If you do not squash that ant at once, it might grow into a snake, or even a dragon.

MASNAVI II:3467; 3472

THE TROUBLED heart is not comforted by lies:
Water and oil produce no light.
Only the truth brings comfort:
Truths are the bait that attracts the heart.

MASNAVI II:2735–6

L EADERSHIP IS a poison except to the one who possesses the antidote in his heart.

MASNAVI II:3464

M ALICE ORIGINATES in hell, and as your malice is a part of hell, it is the enemy of your religion which urges you toward heaven. Since in the grip of malice you are also a part of hell, take care! The part gravitates toward the whole.

MASNAVI II:274–5

WHOEVER SOWS the seed of thistles in this world,
Be warned! Do not look for him in the rose-garden!

MASNAVI II:153

THE PERSON who acquires religious knowledge so that he can show off and increase his popularity, rather than for spiritual enlightenment, is as bad as the seeker of worldly knowledge. Such knowledge is insubstantial and soulless, and its owner complains when no one wants to listen since he loves nothing better than an audience. This kind of knowledge is worldly, and does not bring spiritual freedom.

MASNAVI II:2429–31; 2436

EVEN IF you do not have the same fault as another, do not be complacent; perhaps later it will be yours. You have not heard God's reassurance, "Do not be afraid," so why do you feel so content with yourself? Iblis had a good reputation for years, but in the end he was disgraced, and his fame turned to infamy. Until your own beard grows, do not jeer at the man whose chin is smooth.

MASNAVI II:3038–43

WHAT EXCUSES do you have to offer, my heart, for so many shortcomings? Such constancy on the part of the Beloved, such unfaithfulness on my own!

So much generosity on His side, on mine such niggling contrariness! So much grace from Him, so many faults committed by me!

Such envy, such evil imaginings and dark thoughts in my heart, such drawing, such tasting, such munificence by Him!

Why all this tasting? That my bitter soul may become sweet. Why all this drawing? That I may join the company of the saints.

I am repentant of my sins, I have the name of God on my lips; in that moment He draws me on, so that He may deliver me alive!

DIVAN-I SHAMS 1

TESTS AND SUFFERING

THIS HARSH discipline and rough treatment are a furnace to extract the dross from the silver. This testing purifies the silver; when boiling, the scum rises to the surface.

MASNAVI I:232–3

HUMAN BEINGS are like untanned hide: apply bitter acids and rub them in vigorously and the leather will become soft and supple and full of beauty. Similarly, if you tan the human soul with harsh discipline and suffering, it will gradually become pure, lovely, and very strong. But if you cannot mortify yourself, accept the sufferings God sends you, for afflictions sent by the Friend are the means of your purification. The medicine becomes palatable to the sick when they focus on their health.

MASNAVI IV:104–8

THE FIRE that tempers iron or gold –
    can it be good for fresh quinces and apples?
The apple and quince are only slightly unripe;
    unlike iron, they need a gentle heat.
But gentle flames are not enough for iron;
    it eagerly draws to itself the fiery dragon's heat.
That iron is the dervish who bears hardship:
    under the hammer and fire, he happily glows red.
He goes into the very heart of the fire.

MASNAVI II:827–31

THE SUFFERING in the next world is beyond description. By comparison the suffering needed in this world to prepare yourself for the next is light. Happy are those who immerse themselves in the suffering required for spiritual purification, and who take willingly upon themselves the pain of serving God, and thereby mitigate the pain of the next world.

MASNAVI II:2472–4

WHEN GOD wishes to help, He lets us weep;
But tears for His sake bring happiness,
   and laughter will follow.
Whoever foresees this is a servant of God.
Wherever water flows, life flourishes:
Wherever tears fall, divine mercy is shown.

MASNAVI I:817–20

WHEN GOD assigns a particular lot to a person, this does not preclude him from exercising consent, desire, and free will. But when God sends suffering, the spiritually weak react by fleeing from God; the lovers of God react by moving closer to Him. In battle all fear death, but the cowards choose to retreat while the brave charge toward the enemy. Fear carries the courageous forward, but the weak-spirited die in themselves. Suffering and fear are touchstones: they distinguish the brave from the cowards.

MASNAVI IV:2914–20

GOD CREATED pain and sorrow
    so that happiness is clearly shown in contrast;
For hidden things are made manifest
    by means of their opposites:
Since God has no opposite, He is hidden.

MASNAVI I:1130–1

A certain WOMAN bore a son every year, but he never lived more than six months; he would perish within three months or four.

The woman lamented, saying, "Alas, O God, for nine months I bear the burden and for three months I have joy. My bliss vanishes more swiftly than a rainbow."

Because of the anguish she suffered, the woman complained before the men of God. Twenty sons went to the grave in this way; their lives were consumed by a swift fire.

Then one night she had a vision of an everlasting garden, verdant and delectable. The woman became intoxicated by the sight. She saw her name inscribed upon a palace; being of deep faith, she knew that it was hers.

Thereafter they said to her, "This blessing is reserved for those who have dedicated their lives truly to the service of God, and are thus worthy to partake of this repast. Since you were slow to take shelter with God, God instead bestowed on you these afflictions."

"Lord," she cried, "give me such afflictions for a hundred years and more! Shed my blood!"

When she entered the garden, she saw there all her children.

"They were lost to me," she cried, "but they were not lost to You."

MASNAVI III:3399–415

WEEP LIKE the waterwheel, that green herbs may spring
up from the courtyard of your soul.

MASNAVI I:821–2

WHEN YOU feel pain, give thanks to God, for this pain, in
His hands, is beneficial.
When He pleases, pain becomes joy, and fetters
become freedom.

MASNAVI I:836–7

THERE IS no absolute evil in the world:
evil is relative.
In this world, there is no poison or sugar
that is not a help to one, a hindrance to another.
Snake-poison is life to the snake,
but it is death to a human being.
The sea is paradise to fish,
but can drown animals.

MASNAVI IV:65–9

IF YOU beat a porcupine with a stick, it becomes large and fat. The more you beat it, the more it thrives. The true believer's soul is like a porcupine, for it grows stronger and sturdier the more it is beaten by the blows of suffering. This is why God inflicts greater abasement and suffering on the prophets than on other people.

MASNAVI IV:97–100

WE HAVE the storehouses of everything, and We send it down in certain measure. Without water, earth cannot become a brick, neither can it become a brick when there is too much water.

MASNAVI II:PROLOGUE

HE ALONE has the right to break, for He alone can mend what is broken. He that knows how to sew together, knows how to tear apart: whatever He sells, He buys something better in exchange. He lays the house in ruins: then in a moment He makes it more habitable than before. Since He mends what is broken, His breaking is in reality mending.

MASNAVI I:3882–6

FAITH BRINGS relief to the heart from pain and suffering,
Weakness of faith leads to despair and torment.

MASNAVI II:599

YOUR BITTER cruelty transforms me into a pearl, O
   Spirit!
For pearls and corals dwell in the sea's bitterness.

DIVAN-I SHAMS 21869

BEHOLD THE struggle of the porters with the load! Such is the effort of he who sees the truth of things. Burdens are the foundation of ease, and bitter things are the forerunners of enjoyment. Paradise is encompassed with things we dislike to do, while the fires of hell are encircled with our desires.

MASNAVI II:1835–7

SORROW PREPARES you for joy. It violently sweeps everything out of your house, so that new joy can find space to enter. It shakes the yellow leaves from the bough of your heart, so that fresh, green leaves can grow in their place. It pulls up the rotten roots, so that new roots hidden beneath have room to grow. Whatever sorrow shakes from your heart, far better things will take their place.

MASNAVI V:3678–83

LOOK AT every animal from the gnat to the elephant: all are members of God's family, and dependent on Him for their nourishment. What an excellent provider God is! All these griefs within our hearts arise from the vapor and dust of our existence and vain desires.

MASNAVI I:2295–6

Do not despair, be cheerful, call for help to the One who comes to the call, saying, "Forgive us, You who love to forgive."

MASNAVI I:3252–3

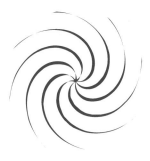

THOUGH DESTINY waylays you a hundred times,
In the end it pitches a tent for you in heaven.
It is God's loving-kindness to terrify you
In order to lead you to the kingdom of safety.

MASNAVI I:1260–1

WHEREVER THE candle of suffering has been lit,
    hundreds of thousands of loving souls are burnt.
Those lovers who are near to God,
    are like moths to the candle of His face.
O heart, go where souls are sincere toward you,
    and can be your coat of mail against suffering,
    and give you a place in their hearts,
    that they can fill you with the wine of love, like a cup.
They will open the book of the soul,
    and reveal the hidden mysteries to you.
Take up your place in their souls!
Make your home in the sky!

MASNAVI II:2574–8

THE UNBELIEVER imagines that he has hurt me,
But no, he has wiped the dust from my mirror.

MASNAVI II:2094

THE EFFECTS and fruits of God's mercy are manifest
    everywhere,
But who knows and understands its essence but God?

MASNAVI III:3635

SELECTED READING

The Mathnawi of Jalalu'ddin Rumi, ed. and trans. R. A. Nicholson, 8 vols, including notes and commentary. London: Luzac, 1925–40

Selected Poems from the Divani Shamsi Tabriz, trans. R. A. Nicholson. Cambridge: Cambridge University Press, 1898, 1961

Discourses of Rumi, trans. A. J. Arberry. London: John Murray, 1961

Mystical Poems of Rumi, vol. I, trans. A. J. Arberry. Chicago: The University of Chicago Press, 1968

Mystical Poems of Rumi, vol. II, trans. A. J. Arberry. Chicago: The University of Chicago Press, 1979

Rumi, Poet and Mystic, trans. R. A. Nicholson. Oxford: Oneworld Publications, 1995

Tales of Mystic Meaning: Selections from the Mathnawi of Jalal-ud-Din Rumi, trans. R. A. Nicholson. Oxford: Oneworld Publications, 1995

Rumi – Past and Present, East and West, Franklin D. Lewis. Oxford: Oneworld Publications, 2000

Sufism: A Short Introduction, William C. Chittick. Oxford: Oneworld Publications, 2000